Table of Content

CHAPTER ONE

WHAT DOES THE BIBLE SAY ABOUT PRAYER?

"Do not be anxious about anything, but in every situation, by prayer and petition, with thanksgiving, present your requests to God."

Philippians 4:6

Prayer is the act of communicating and connecting with God. However, it is not just an activity as we often perceive, rather, it is a lifestyle and a fundamental part of the nature of God in us. Prayer is a powerful experience that cannot be stereotyped (that is, limited to a specific setting or hour), determined or defined. As Christians, for us to maintain an effective and efficient prayer life, it is important to study and understand what the bible says about prayer. What is prayer?

The first thing that you must understand is that prayer is not an act of speaking to the air or producing some random or specific utterances as we have been taught to do? It is an act of conversing with God. Prayer is the state where humanity engages divinity to produce results initially deemed impossibility. Jesus said in Luke 18:1 that **man ought to pray and not faint**. In Jeremiah 33:3, we hear God say "Call to me and I will answer you **and tell you great and unsearchable things** you do not know." More so, Apostle Paul admonishes us in 1 Thessalonians 5: 16-18 to **pray without ceasing**.

"Man Ought to Pray and not Faint"

__Jesus Christ (Luke 18:1)

Here, Jesus is saying prayer is not suppose to be an activity exclusive to certain team (prayer team) in the church or limited only to specific hours of the day, it should be a lifestyle, a default character of a child of God. When prayer is increasingly boring and difficult for you, it is either you don't have the right standing with God or your heart is distracted by the temporal pleasures of a fading and perishing world. What Jesus is saying here is that man ought to live life consistently connected to heaven. We are not created to walk this planet alone. From the beginning of the world, God has never abandoned man. We are His most esteem creation. When Adam sinned and lost the presence of God, God wouldn't give up on us him, rather He reached out to man with His enduring kindness. Down to our days, God still sends angels, raise prophets and preachers, come through visions and dreams, etc to reach out to us. This is because a life disconnected from God cannot accomplish His purpose. In Luke 18:1, Jesus wants us to see prayer not as an option or an activity to engage in at our convenience. It is part of what makes us a complete man. This is like saying birds ought to fly, lions ought to roar, fish ought to swim etc. When you see an eagle unable to fly, a lion that cannot roar or a fish that cannot swim, then something terrible must have happened. When you see a man that cannot pray, something incredibly dangerous has happened to that man because Prayer is meant to be a default character of a child of God. I love the way Charles Spurgeon puts it:

> *"So deep are our necessities, that until we are in heaven we must not cease to pray. Dost thou want nothing? Then, I fear thou dost not know thy poverty. Hath thou no mercy to ask of God? Then, may the Lord's mercy show thee thy misery! A prayerless soul is a Christless soul. Prayer is the lisping of the believing infant, the shout of the fighting believer, the requiem of the dying saint falling asleep in Jesus. It is the breath, the watchword, the comfort, the strength, the honour of a Christian."*

__God (Jeremiah 33:3)

And I will answer you and tell you great and unsearchable things

__God (Jeremiah 33:3)

Prayer is conversational. This is an aspect of praying that is often unexplored by many children of God. We either lack the understanding or the patience to hear from God each time we kneel to pray. One reason why prayer can be very boring and tiring is when it becomes a creed, repetition, or one **"man talk."** Imagine going to your father to ask a lot of things and without waiting for his reply, you just bang the door and leave. Even if your father generously grants your request, he is not likely satisfied with the rude way you related with him. This is the same way it works with our Father and Lord. It is rude and inconsiderate to talk to God without allowing Him to talk to us. God reveals that through prayer, we have an exciting moment of communion with Him and through that interaction; we have revelation of life and eternity. Through prayers the deep mysteries of God become explicit; we receive direction and understanding for life. Therefore, prayer is not an activity but a relationship between you and your Maker.

Who Should Pray?

We have established so far that prayer is a sacred privilege and a default character of a child of God. However, it is obvious that not everyone can pray or should pray. While some people find it too demanding, some finds it ineffective. Although prayer was originally wired into the nature of man, the fall of Adam has corrupted the seed of God in us. A natural man is a fallen man and by all standards, he is short of the glory of God. This is why James 5: 16 says "confess your sins … [for] the effectual prayer of the righteous man avails much." A man fondling with sin cannot enjoy the sanctity and spirituality of prayer. When he prays, he feels the void and the emptiness in his heart. Usually, he would abandon the place of prayer to find answers elsewhere. This is because God is holy and a sinful man cannot enter into or stand in His presence. Isaiah 59: 1-2 expose a very important secret of prayer by saying: *"Surely the arm of the LORD is not too short to save, nor His ear too dull to hear. But your iniquities have built barriers between you and your God, and your sins have hidden His face from you, so that He will not hear."* There is a part of us that is always yearning for answers from God and there is a part of God that is reaching out to us but sin is a strong barrier. A man given to sin and lust is leading a detached life from God which is not without eternal consequences. Beloved child of God, your Father wants to walk and work with you in a way eyes have not seen, ears have not heard nor entered into the heart of man. But before God can get the glory out of your life, He demands your worship and submission. He wants to be the LORD and Saviour of your life. There is much to which God can do with a life that is surrendered to Him. If you want to unleash the unlimited power of God, you must drop your life at His feet and allow Him to lead it the way He pleases.

Prayer Points:

- Dear Lord, as I seek Your face today, I pray that you will enlighten my heart to understand the meaning and privilege of prayer.
- Give me the strength to seek your face without getting tired or bored.
- Help me to spend more time in pray and empower me to love Your presence.

Chapter Two

The Power of Prayer

Many Believers do not know the weight and greatness of the privilege of praying. Unfortunately for some Believers, prayer has become a normal routine or a set of utterances mastered and recited. How come this sacred creed of the saints has become so ineffective and inefficient? We claim to swing the strongest sword of spiritual warfare, yet we are slaving under the tyranny of sin, sickness and Satan. Have you forgotten Elijah, who through prayer rained fire from heaven and cease rain from the earth for years? Joshua commanded the sun to stand still, Moses parted the sea, Jesus raised the dead, the Apostles of old cast out demons and heal the sick and all of these were done through the agency of prayer. How come in our days, prayer has become so habitual and devoid of power?

James 5:16 makes it clear that the effectual fervent prayer of a righteous man avails much. Do you think it was a joke when Jesus said in Matthew 17: 20 that "if you have faith as a mustard seed, you will say to this mountain, 'Move from here to there,' and it will move; **and nothing shall be impossible unto you."** Weird as it might sound; Jesus actually means there is nothing your prayers cannot do. You can avert death, you can attract success, you can obtain promises, and rewrite history through a simple act of prayer. It is often said that a prayer-less man is a powerless man. There is mighty power at the disposal of a man who knows the secret place of power. Men of prayer are feared by kings, sorted after by nations and honored by demons. This is because they hold constant conference with the Supreme God, the uncreated Creator of the Universe.

We will like to establish, at this juncture, that prayer is an untamable force of God reacting upon an ordinary man to produce extraordinary results. A faithless heart will fail in the place of prayer but when the prayer of a righteous man is powered on the wings of faith, Heaven must respond with resounding speed and answers. The reason why some people are defeated in their walk with God, why that sickness is lingering in their lives, why there is no breakthrough in business etc. is because they have not collided with the prayer powered by faith. Jesus specifically mentions the unimaginable power available when we pray with faith. Mark 11: 24 says "I tell you, **whatever** you ask for in prayer, **believe that you have it,** and it will be yours." Hope you take note of the **"whatever"** in the statement of Jesus? Does that mean there is nothing impossible through prayer? Yes! That is how powerful your prayers can be. Do not forget that Jesus also says **you must believe.** That is where faith comes in.

In Hebrews 11:33-34, we read about how men of faith and prayer "subdued kingdoms, wrought righteousness, obtained promises, stopped the mouths of lions, quenched the violence of fire, escaped the edge of the sword, were made strong out of weakness, waxed valiant in fight and turned to flight the armies of aliens."

Maybe there are unsorted issues in your life that keeps you bothered. It might be related to your home, career, business or ministry. You might have known the harsh tyranny of sin and sickness, and the storm of this passing life might be rising above your head. I speak peace to your life right now and I release you to experience the limitless power of God. Join me in this sacred spot of the spirit where men of noble feet had walked, stand with me in the place of prayer, keep your faith and you shall see the greatness of your God.

☐ Prayer Point: My Father and my God, thank You for the wisdom of your word. Thank you for the power of Prayer.

Chapter Three

Stages of Prayer

As we have earlier pointed out in this book, prayer is the sacred engagement of the supernatural, a point of convergence between divinity and humanity. There are different stages of prayer and as we keenly pay attention to the Word of God and observe in our walk with the Lord over the years, we have discovered that there are three stages of prayer. We will conceptualize these stages in simple and unsophisticated terms.

Stage One: Natural Stage

The natural stage of prayer is the first stage of prayer when we are still very conscious of our natural lives, physical environment and surrounding events. This is the first and very critical stage of prayer. Prayer is a spiritual activity and those who pray must do so in truth and in the spirit (Ephesians 6:18, John 4:24). As we kneel or stand in prayer, our intention is to commune with God which involves become less sensitive to your physical environment and aligning our focus with the reality of the Spirit. This is like standing at the door of the holies of holies. The kind of life you have will determine if you will cross to the next stage of prayer. At this point, you will discover that we can be easily distracted, our minds might wander around and it often takes discipline to concentrate. Not many people make it through this stage. As many people stand at this entrance, which is the first stage, the Holy Spirit would remind them of **"un-repented,"** the grudges or malice in their heart, the unholy things they are involved in etc. You will discover that at this point, it is very possible to be discouraged and defeated. Before you are allowed to enter into the presence of God, your life will be checked and examined. Jesus in Matthew 5:23 says if you are at the altar and you remember you have unsorted issues in your life, leave whatever you are doing and first make right your ways. We said in Chapter One that a defiled life is a detached life. When your heart is disturbed and distracted, you cannot engage the Deity of the Divine. Do you know that this is the reason why so many people have lost faith in prayer? Because they have prayed but there were no answers. Actually, those whose prayers are limited to this stage will always doubt the potency of prayer because they are at the door.

Many Christians today are like the seven sons of Sceva (Acts 19:15). They were unqualified to enter into the holy presence of God because of the quality of life they lived. They wanted to cast out demons and see results. "Eventually, one of the evil spirits answered them, 'Jesus I know, Paul I know, but who are you?" The demon pounced on them, overpowered them and gave them the beating of their lives. Beloved child of God, have you made peace with your God? When you stand at the entrance of the holies of holies, do you have the consecrated life that will allow you in? If you are not, you can turn to God right now and settle it with God. When you kneel in prayer and you remember how you have been unfaithful to your vows and to His words, would you stand up and leave the matter unfinished or will you tell Him you are sorry and willing to yield your life to His will?

Mental Stage

We call this stage mental because it is a middle ground between the physical and the spiritual. This wonderful stage is the stage of transition in our emotions as we find connection with the Divine presence of God. At this point, we are losing our grip on the physical consciousness and beginning to have a glimpse of the glory of God. This is difficult to explain but as you pray, you will remember that there are times when your heart is lifted and you feel His fresh presence around you. O, this is a beautiful experience that brings both joy and trembling. It is not the final stage, we are still in control of our actions and we are still partly aware of what happens around us. This is the point where we experience the kind of power described in Philippians 3: 21' Jesus encourages us to "transform the body of our humble state into conformity with the body of His glory, by the exertion of the power that He has even to subject all things to Himself."

This stage is an exclusive stage for the children of God. No random person can access this stage except He is first admitted into the family of our King. A genuine child of God must reach this stage each time he/she kneels down to pray.

Spiritual Stage

The last stage is simply called the spiritual stage and as the name implies, it is a state of great insensitivity to the physical environment and a deep consciousness of the presence of God. This is the Pentecostal kind of experience. Are there not times you pray so deeply that you are totally unaware of what happens around you? You are simply caught up in the spirit into the presence of God. This stage might not be commonly experience but it is real. It is the deepest stage and it can last for hours.

Jesus consistently experienced this during His earthly Ministry. This is what Luke 6:12 says: "In those days, Jesus went out to the mountain to pray, and He spent the night in prayer to God." Several other Scriptures like Luke 9:18, Luke 5:16, Mark 3:13 etc. makes it clear that Jesus often detach Himself from the crowd including His disciples to be alone with God and many of these times, He prays all night. How can a wandering heart stay in prayer for 12 hours? This is to tell you that Jesus was not just producing utterances, He was having a meeting with God.

The mental stage leads us into the spiritual stage where we are no longer in control of how long or brief we stay in the place of prayer. At the mental stage, we have a glimpse of the glory of the spiritual stage and as we behold with an unveiled face as in a mirror the glory of the Lord, we are transformed into the same image from glory to glory, just as the Lord, the Spirit (2 Corinthians 3:18). When a man frequents this realm on the wings of prayer, his life will not be determined by the immutable laws of nature. When you see Jesus walking on water, the Apostles raising the dead etc., this is because they are known in the court yard of God where the fullness of His glory tabernacles.

Understanding these three stages will guide you to pray. The first stage is the point where you know if you are qualified to enter into the Holies of Holies. The second stage is the emotional state of perceiving God. There is a measure of power at this stage but one must consciously release himself/herself to the consuming presence of God. The third stage cannot be defined and explained in words. It is simply the overwhelming experience of God, an encounter that leaves man with a definite mark of God's presence.

Prayer Points: Dear:

- Dear Lord, please help my heart to pray the way I ought.
- Take away all forms of hindrances in my life to prayer.
- Keep my heart from wandering in prayer and help me to stay focus on You each time I pray.

Chapter Four

How to Pray

Did you know that prayer has an approved approach by God? James 4:3 says *"when you ask, you do not receive because you asked amiss."* It is possible to pray and yet not pray correctly. In this Chapter, we will look at the Scriptures to understand the mind of God on how to pray.

Amazingly, in Luke 11:1, the disciples asked Jesus this same question. *"One day Jesus was praying in a certain place. When he finished, one of his disciples said to Him, "Lord, teach us to pray, just as John taught his disciples."* The Lord replied by teaching them a method of prayer which is now known as the Lord's Prayer. The Lord's Prayer, as we will find out is not just a creed to be recited or a portion of the bible to be memorized, it is a method of prayer taught, practiced and approved by our Lord Jesus Christ.

*"After this manner therefore pray ye: Our Father
which art in heaven, Hallowed be thy name*

*Thy Kingdom come. Thy will be done in earth, as
it is in heaven.*

Give us this day our daily bread.

*And forgive us our debts as we forgive our
debtors*

*And lead us not into temptation, but deliver us
from evil: for thine is the kingdom, and the power
and the glory, forever. Amen."*

Matthew 6: 9-13

Our Father

God does not want us to pray a directionless prayer. The first thing to do in prayer is to address to whom you are praying. We are all children of God and we are to address Him as our Father. We are not to approach the Throne of God with the mind of an outcast. *"For we do not receive the spirit of slavery that returns you to fear, but you received the Spirit of sonship, by whom we cry Abba! Father! The Spirit Himself testifies with our spirit that we are God's children. And if we are children, then we are heirs: heirs of God and co-heirs with Christ"* (Romans 8:15-17). Again, we see that prayer is based on relationship and not just activity. Jesus says when we pray, we should say "Our Father." You cannot call a stranger "Father." It is a congenial relationship mutually acknowledge by both parties. It is not right to feel rejected in the presence of God and Jesus wouldn't want us to approach the throne of our Father with that mentality. The awareness of being children of God should not only be activated when we want to pray, we ought to live and walk in this consciousness daily.

Hallowed Be Thy Name

The next step after addressing our prayer to God is to give Him thanks and worship Him for who He's and all He's done. We should not abuse the privilege of accessing God. We are to acknowledge for who He is and be grateful for His unwavering commitment towards us. We must worship and adore Him in prayer.

Thy Kingdom Come, Thy will be Done

In Matthew 6:33, Jesus admonishes us to seek first the kingdom of God and His righteousness. This is reflected in the way our Lord Jesus prays. You will remember one of His prayer in the Garden of Gethsemane was "Father, not my will, but your will be done." We must pray in the understanding of God's will. You must check if what you are about to ask in prayer are in alignment with His will for you. Many times, we do not receive because we ask amiss. As Christians, Jesus is our Lord so we should allow Him chart the course of our destinies by surrendering to Him in faith. Our prayer should not be out of vain desperation or competition, but for the glory of God.

Give Us Our Daily Bread

After acknowledging God for who He is, thanking Him for what he has done, and seeking His will, you can now ask what you need. It is not a crime to ask Him for our deepest desires. The Creator of Heaven and Earth is our Father and as we read in Philippians 4:19, He shall "supply all our need according to His riches in glory by Christ Jesus."

Forgive Us Our Trespasses as We have Forgiven others

Do not expect to receive speedy answers when your heart is embittered against someone. You cannot be plotting someone's downfall and expect God to lift you up. In the place of prayer, there is nothing wrong in admitting that you are just an ordinary man and not beyond mistakes. We are not angels and there are sometimes we find ourselves failing at certain areas. It might be a simple disobedience to the Holy Spirit; it might be a form of insensitivity to the needs of people around you, a word of unkindness etc. We should always ask for the forgiveness of God and also let go of those things we hold against others. If forgiveness is not a necessary tool for an unhindered prayer, Jesus will not put it dear. But because it is one of those things that open the gate of Heaven for the release of abundant blessings, we must not take it lightly. May God grant you a heart that forgives.

Lead Us Not into Temptation

We should not forget to ask for the release of more grace to run through this life of many temptations. To finish strong in life, there is a grace we must have upon our lives. It is very easy to miss it as a Christian. Many people are now shadows of their destinies, some are defeated victims and enslaved under the tyranny of sin. There is a grace needed for exploit in the will of God and we must deliberately ask for this grace.

Pray the Word

"For Thine is the kingdom, the power and the glory forever." When you pray, it is always a very good practice to pray with the Word of God. The Word serves as an anchor and a ground to establish ourselves upon the promises of God. God says "I exalt My word above My name." The word of God is a powerful instrument that must not be found wanting as we pray.

Prayer Points:

- Dear Lord, I thank you for the privilege of prayer and the opportunity to commune with you.
- As I pray, guide my lips and help my heart to pray approvingly.
- Forgive and remove all forms of hindrances that is preventing me from accessing the presence of God.
- Help me from today to live a prayerful life.

Chapter Five

Prayer vs Intercession

Prayer is a formidable weapon of a Believer. An unguided Christian who is not armed with the act of prayer will become a cheap prey for the enemy to devour. He can be easily defeated, manipulated, victimized, abused and oppressed. Prayer is not an indispensable element for a man who desires to finish strong in life.

Although we have all the right to invite God into our situations and take absolute charge of our lives, it is of great importance to understand that we are not supposed to use this most esteemed privilege for granted. God expects us to leverage of this divine privilege to become a channel of blessing to the world

We will talk on the prayer of intercession later in this book, but we want to quickly establish that interceding for others in this world is one of our most important duties as Children of God. We are governors of this realm and custodians of the power and greatness of God. God decries the decreasing number of intercessors in Ezekiel 22:30 by saying *"I looked for someone among them who would build up the wall and stand before me in the gap on behalf of the land so that I would not have to destroy it, but I found no one."*

Could it be that God is still looking for intercessors in our generation today? You can be a channel through which the world will feel the power of God by standing in gap for them through prayer today.

Prayer Points:

- My Lord, I am grateful for the gift of life and the grace to come before you once again.
- I pray, this day, that you will help me to always stand in gap for those you have placed around me.
- Let it not be that you will keep looking for intercessors when I am alive.
- Make me powerful in prayer so that I can do exploit for Your kingdom.

Chapter Nine

The Power of the Secret of Place

"But when you pray, go into your inner room,
close your door and pray to your Father who is in
secret, and your Father who sees what is done in
secret will reward you."

Matthew 6:6

The secret place of prayer is the place of power where the battles of life are won. The greatest victories ever known in the history of our faith are won on the knees. Anytime you see a man waxing strong in Christ daily, he must have known the secret of that precious time alone with God. There are storms and conflicts in the world but a man of prayer has his victory secured. As a Christian, our battles are not won on the field, they are won on the knees. Our victories are gained in the closet. This is why

Jesus encourages us to go into the inner room, behind closed doors and pray to our Father.

Many times during the ministry of Jesus, we see Him withdraw from the crowd to the mountains or caves where He prays alone with God. At times He sends people away just to be alone. He had a very busy schedule as an itinerant preacher but He wouldn't allow anything to rob Him of a personal time with His Father. Cooperate and congregational prayers are very good and encouraged, but God wants us to withdraw from the crowd frequently to be with Him. Bob Sorge observed that "nothing is more dangerous to the kingdom of darkness than a man or woman who has found the unceasing wellspring of heaven." Men of prayer are men of power. Those who know how to kneel before God can stand before any man.

How do you manage the storms and confusions of life? Do you frequently withdraw from the crowd to spend time with God? Do you have a personal altar or a secret place where you engage God for the release of His power? Look at the patriarchs and matriarchs of our faith for instance; they were men of the secret place. The sea could not stop Moses, the fiery furnace will not burn the three Hebrew boys (Meshach Shadrach and Abednego), the hungry lions became friends with Daniel, the mighty walls of Jericho fell flat before Joshua, the mantle of Elijah parted Jordan, the bones of Elisha raised the dead, the shadows of Peter healed the sick and the list goes on. The secret place is the place where spiritual heat and intensity is generated for exploit and the power of God is released in the fullest measure.

Prayer Points:

1. Dear Lord, help me to love the secret place.
2. I have learnt that a life of power is only possible to a man of prayer; help me stay ablaze for you in the place of prayer.

Chapter Seven

Prayer of Thanksgiving

O Give thanks unto the LORD, for He is good: for His mercy endures forever.

Psalms 107: 1

Today, we will look at one very important aspect of prayer. The Prayer of Thanksgiving is an act of thanking God, appreciating Him for His loving kindness and giving Him the glory that only Him deserves. Prayer is not always about what we can get from God all the time. We should also learn to say *"thank you"* for all He has done or yet to do. Saying thank you to God should be a very important aspect of our daily prayer. His ultimate sacrifice on the cross that we might be redeemed from death and destruction and reconciled back to God is more than enough reason why we should thank Him. How about His protection, provision and mercy? Take a look at your life, you will see more than enough reason to thank God for who He is and what He's done.

Thanking God is not a conditional thing. Even when things are bad; a wise Believer will still have the courage to say thank you Jesus. Apostle Paul counsel in 1 Thessalonians 5:18 that "in everything give thanks: for this is the will of God in Christ Jesus concerning you." If we are patient enough to count and number our blessings, we will see more than enough reason to thank Him.

The gift of salvation is more than what money can buy. How about the gift of life, provision and protection? Although God is not man, but thanking God for what He has done can encourage Him to do more. Even though our God is good and gracious, He loves it when His people acknowledge His kindness by not taking it for granted or as a right. Why not take a moment today to say thank you Jesus.

Prayer Points:

▪ Lord Jesus, I thank You for the gift of salvation and freedom from the oppression of sin.

▪ I appreciate your Holy name for all you have given to me. For the gift of life, for provision, for protection.

▪ I cannot exhaust the list of your kindness but I am grateful for your love and commitment over my life these many years.

▪ Receive all the glory and honour and glory now and forever more. Amen.

Chapter Eight

Prayer of Blessing and Adoration

Exalt the LORD our God and worship at His holy mountain, for the LORD our God is holy.

Psalm 99:9

Who else is worthy of our praises if not God? He deserves our worship not just because He is our God but because He is our savior. It is a beautiful and soul lifting practice to worship God for whom He is. We are to bow in humble adoration before the Maker of Heaven and Earth. God is glorious; He is a mystery too deep to understand, too mighty to comprehend, too holy to approach, too righteous to fault. The saints above and the host of angels worship Him who is seated upon the throne forever. We read in Revelation 4:8 that the "four beasts who have six wings each and are full of eyes rest not day and night, saying Holy, holy,

holy Lord God Almighty, which was, and his and is to come. More so, Revelation 4: 10-11 reveals that:

> *"Whenever the living creatures give glory, honor and thanks to the One seated on the throne who lives forever and ever, the twenty-four elders fall down before the One seated on the throne, and they worship Him who lives forever and ever. They cast their crowns before the throne, saying: "You are worthy, our Lord and God, to receive glory and honour and power, for You have created all things; by Your will they exist, and came to be."*

Praying the prayer of adoration and praise is teaming up with the host of heaven and the saints of God in glory to acknowledge the greatness of our King. Our Lord Jesus teaches us to say, ***"Hallowed be Thy name."*** We should not be carried away by the activities of this fading world and forget the act of worshiping God in prayer. In worship, miracles happen, chains are broken, yokes are removed, the captives are set free, and the sick are made whole.

"Give unto the LORD, ye kindred of the people, give unto the LORD glory and strength" (1 Chronicles 16:28, 29). He alone deserves our praises. When we allow our hearts to worship God, we see His supremacy over our situations and His ability to take control of the storms in our lives. However, the moment we shift our gaze from His glory and dwell on our challenges, we are easily enslaved and entangled by the cares of life. The prayer of worship is the prayer of absolute surrender and a declaration of the unlimited greatness of God. "Worthy is the Lamb who was slain, to receive power and riches and wisdom and strength and honour and glory and blessing" (Revelation 5:12). Today, we shall take a moment to just to worship God. He alone deserves our praises.

Prayer Points:

- My Father and my God, today I just want to bless and adore you for who you are.
- I build you a throne of praise and I humble myself before you my King.
- Your glory is un-ending and your love endures forever more.

Chapter Nine

Prayer of Petition

What is Petition? The literal meaning of the word petition, according to the Cambridge Dictionary, is a formal letter or a document signed by a large number of people asking for some action from the government or authorities. When we talk about the Prayer of Petition, we are simply implying the act of going to God to make a request that demands actions either for ourselves or on behalf of others. The act of petitioning involves two parties: the higher authority and the people. For instance, as the petitioner approaches the government, he does so with confidence in the ability of the government. He acknowledges the supremacy and the ability of the government.

One thing is sacrosanct when we pray the prayer of petition; we must come to God not only with our request but in faith and recognition of

His power. Apostle Paul reveals that "without faith it is impossible to please God, because anyone who approaches Him must believe that He exists and that He rewards those who earnestly seek Him" (Hebrews 11: 6).

There could be several issues in your life today that needs to get to the throne of God, it might be a sick relative, a misbehaving spouse or child, a stunted business etc, "this is the confidence we have in approaching God: that if we ask anything according to his will, he hears us. If we know that He hears us; whatever we ask, we know that we have what we asked of Him." (1 John 5: 14-15).

Today is another day to approach the throne of grace with all the challenges in your life. Come to the feet of Jesus, look upon His strength and seek His face, for only He can do what no man can do.

Prayer Points:

- Dear Lord, I believe there is nothing impossible for you to do. I come before you in this confidence and I table before you the challenges of my life.
- (List out the things you want God to do for your and pray about them in the assurance that God will answer.)

Chapter Ten

PRAYER OF SUPPLICATION

Be careful for nothing; but in everything by

prayer and supplication with thanksgiving let your

request be made known unto God.

Phillipians 4:6

A prayer of supplication is a prayer of request unto God and it has much affinity with the prayer of petition. When we humble ourselves before the Most High to earnestly make a request, we are making a prayer of supplication.

Being humble and having faith are prerequisite in making this kind of. Apostle Paul admonishes us to be anxious for nothing, but rather make our requests known to God through prayers. In other words, we should not be impatient to have our requests granted but instead to wait in the peace of God which surpasses all understanding to guard our hearts and minds through Jesus Christ. This means all that we desire and require as believers are embedded in the words of life - God [John 1:1], God will open our eyes to knowledge, wisdom, understanding, skills, help etc.

Are there pressing needs in your life today? At the presence of God, all forms of hopelessness terminate. You are a child of God and you should go boldly before the throne of God in humility. God wants to hear your pleasing voice and respond to your pressing needs today.

Prayer Points

- Heavenly Father, I ask in the name of Jesus Christ to please bless, heal, restore and promote me.
- Make me a good follower of your words and commandments, who satisfies your heart desires at all time.
- (Mention the specific areas in your life that you want the intervention of God.)

Chapter Eleven

PRAYER OF REPENTANCE AND FORGIVENESS

Read Psalm 51: 1-15

We are living in an imperfect world and we sometimes find ourselves compromising some of God's standards. Sometimes, we can be provoked by people to get angry and act in an unpleasant way, some of our pursuits and desires can be selfish, we might find it difficult to forgive someone who has hurt us in the past, etc. the point we are trying to make is that there is always a very good reason to ask for forgiveness in the place of prayer. Our Lord Jesus Christ also taught us to always say: "forgive me my trespasses as I have forgiven those who trespass against me." To pray for repentance and forgiveness means to acknowledge that you are imperfect and you need the mercy from God to keep a renewed spirit.

Repentance is the condition of being penitent, feeling pain, sorrow or regret for what one has done or failed to do. Forgiveness on the other hand is the act of forgiving, to pardon and waive any negative feeling or desire to punish. We offer repentance while God offers love, forgiveness and restoration.

It is not enough to ask for forgiveness, you must have a repentant heart. For instance, King David after transgressing against Uriah by killing him and having an affair with Bathsheba he was condemned by God through the Prophet Nathan and he acknowledged his sins and repented of them genuinely. [Psalm 51: 1-2].

Prayer Points

- Father, I know I am imperfect and my imperfection can separate me from you. I acknowledge my nothingness before you and I ask for your forgiveness today.
- Grant me a heart that genuinely repent and grant men the grace to go and sin no more.
- Create in me a new heart and renew Thy Spirit within me.

Chapter Twelve

PRAYER OF INTERCESSION

I exhort therefore, that, first of all, supplications, prayers, intercessions, and giving thanks, be made for all men;

1 Timothy 2:1

Prayers of intercession are prayers offered to God on behalf of others. We can pray on behalf of our family members, relatives, friends, co-workers, employees, nation amongst others, even for a cause and most importantly our enemies.

As Christians and Believers of Christ, prayers of intercession are what should be done from time to time. We live in a world perverse to the Kingdom of God, we must constantly pray to God for salvation, the healing and the forgiveness of others. Jesus Christ exemplified this in Luke 23:24 where He prayed for those that mocked Him on the cross of Calvary.

God always wants us to stand in the gap for other people. Fathers are to offer prayers for their children [Genesis 17:18], employees must pray for their employers [Genesis 24:12-24], prayers must be offered to those who transgress against us [2 Timothy 4:16]. We must pray for our nation [Jeremiah 29:7] and those in authority [1Timothy 2:2]. The Bible instructs us to pray in supplication, thanksgiving and intercessions for all men [1Timothy 2:1].

We must learn to spend time praying for others. Prayers of intercessions are powerful. The Bible records that the weather changed, people were released from prison, enemies were defeated, and many more, all as a result of intercessory prayer. Won't you spend time today to talk to God about that person in your life that needs the divine touch of God? Your prayer today can make a difference in their lives. Abraham intercedes for Lot before God and Lot's life was spared. God wants you to stand in the gap for others who cannot pray. Pray for those that are sick, the less privileged, the broken and the lost.

Prayer Points:

- (Identify someone or people in your life that needs the help and mercy of God and pray raise them up in prayer before God.)
- I pray for my country and those in the position of power and prominence, help them to be guided in your will.

⬜ I pray for the missionaries laboring in dark and dangerous fields and spreading the Gospel in heathen lands, strengthen them and provide for their needs.

⬜ I pray for the homeless orphans, bereaved widow or widower, comfort them and be to them more than a man can be.

⬜ Preserve your anointed in your will and keep their feet from slipping.

Chapter Thirteen

PRAYER OF FAITH

Now faith is the substance of things hoped for, the
evidence of things not seen.

Hebrews 11:1

And the prayer of faith shall save the sick.

James 5:15

As the Bible declares "faith is the substance of things hoped for, the evidence of things not seen." Praying by faith implies believing in the ability of God to turn situations around. The most important aspect of this prayer is faith. We must have an unwavering assurance in the ability of God. When your faith says yes, God will not say no.

After making a prayer of faith, we should cheerfully commit our lives into God's hands. The prayer of faith is persistent, we must not get weary if our prayer is not answered immediately. We must be ardent, and consistent in faith. Jesus in Matthew 7:7 implores us to ask and it shall be given, seek and we shall find, knock and it shall be opened unto us. When we refuse to ask and we don't receive. It takes the prayer of faith to move mountains. Without faith, it is impossible to please God.

"Faith is to prayer what the feather is to the arrow: without it prayer will not hit the mark."

- J.C. Ryle.

We must come to God in prayer with a believing heart. We must wait, in faith and with a believing heart knowing well that even though it tarries, the answers will come and it will just be on time. We must trust in the sovereignty of God, prayer of faith is said with absolute confidence that God will answer. I encourage you to come before God with confidence in Him for He will do that which you ask in faith.

Prayer Points

- I command every troubling storm in my life to be calm and I decree every snare of the powers of darkness to cease to manifest in my life.
- I declare peace into my home in the name of Jesus
- I take authority over every situation in my life to the glory of God.

Chapter Fourteen

PRAYER OF CONSECRATION

Do not go on presenting the members of your body to sin as instruments of unrighteousness; but present yourselves to God as those alive from the dead, and your members as instruments of righteousness to God.

Romans 6:13

Your body is the temple of God where His fullness tabernacles. Therefore, you must live a consecrated life, fully separated for the glory of God. To consecrate means to dedicate to a higher authority. Prayer of consecration is an act of praying and trusting God for purification and sanctification of our lives. The Holy Spirit will be limited in operation if we are not purified.

Jesus Christ as we all know lived a life of consecration, his life on earth was meant for a divine purpose. In Luke 22:39-42, we read that Jesus withdrew from the crowd to a stone cast, knelt down and prayed to God to remove the cup from him if God is willing. We know how the story ends, it was God's will for him to bear the cup which Jesus Christ did bear. He wanted to do what God wanted him to do, it wasn't a supplication to get something from God or petition to God to change something. It is simply a separation for a holy course.

Consecration involves total, voluntary surrender to God and His will. In a prayer of consecration, we are saying to God "Use me today", "Speak through me Lord", "Here I am Lord, Unto you I commit myself", "I bring myself to your altar, mould me as you wish", "Use me to meet divine appointments today", "i am available for your plans and purpose Lord".

Prayer of consecration is a prayer to God to change us, transform us and purify us for His glory.

We must know that when we make prayers of consecration, we must be ready to turn our backs to the desires of the world, our earthly desires should be banished to allow God to come into our lives.

Prayer Points

- Dear Lord, my body is Your sanctuary, purify me like gold, so that I might be useful in your hands.
- Lord prepare me as a sanctuary, pure and holy, tried and true. With thanksgiving, I will be a living sanctuary for you.

Chapter Fifteen

WARFARE PRAYER

For we wrestle not against flesh and blood, but
against principalities, against powers, against the
rulers of the darkness of this world, against
spiritual wickedness in high places

Ephesians 6:12

As the name implies, warfare prayer is a kind of prayer used to fight spiritual battles and gain victory over everything that is against God in our lives. It is for waging war against the forces of darkness whose purposes are to hinder progress the believers with chains of sins and sickness.

Do you know that the world is a war zone? A child of God is constantly at war with the camp of the enemy. For we do not wrestle against flesh and blood, but against principalities, against powers, against the rulers of the darkness of this world, against spiritual hosts of wickedness in the heavenly places. The Church on earth is known as the Church Militant while the congregation of saints in heaven is called the Church Triumphant. In other words, as long as we are still down here, we will always have a reason to engage in spiritual warfare.

These are perilous times and the reality in our world is that there are operational forces that want to see the glory of God upon our lives cut short or destroyed. We must therefore take arm in prayers against these enemies of destiny and fulfillment of purpose.

As a Christian, tests and trials are lurking in every corner of our daily lives, we must daily commune with God to strengthen us to overcome such temptations and test of faith, constantly. Starting the day without prayers is like heading out without breakfast, the mortal body is weak without food so is the spiritual body weak and not immune to crisis, soon enough, confusion and weakness set in.

James 5:16 tells us the fervent prayer of a righteous man avails much. This means a Christian who walks upright in God has prayers to his advantage. Spiritual warfare are fought and won through just one weapon __**prayer**. Jesus tells us whatever is bound on earth is also bound in heaven, prayer will help us achieve this, it transcends physical planes into the metaphysical realm. It is our means of sending messages to the Almighty, the doer of all things.

Prayer Points

- Lord, as I begin my day, I pray that You would fill me with Your Holy Spirit. Cover me with your protecting wings and keep me safe from harm and spiritual attacks.
- I take authority over every negative forces in my life and I bring to subjection every knowledge that exalt itself above my God.

Chapter Sixteen

THE ARMOR OF GOD

Read Ephesians 6: 10-18

The armor of God is our spiritual defense against the forces of darkness. Beloved Child of God, we are all at war against an un-aging enemy and this is why we need to constantly guard ourselves with the whole armor of God. Not one, but all. The more we dedicate our lives to God, the more we frustrate the plots of satan When we stand firm in God and in His mighty power, we have nothing to fear.

The question now is "what are the pieces or parts of God's armor?" Apostle Paul in his letter to the Ephesians made this known to us. We are to guard our loins with the Belt of Truth. The belt is what keeps a soldier's armor in place, smart and ever ready. As a child of God, do you allow the truth to be your priority in your day to day life? A life that lacks integrity is unguided and at the mercy of the enemy. Purity holds our spiritual lives and affirms our connection to Christ Jesus. Jesus

Christ says He is Truth, the Way and the Life, what is a believer without the truth?

How about the Breastplate of Righteousness? Righteousness is not an optional character of a believer. Everything we say and do generates from our heart and this is why we must keep a righteous heart. Guard your heart above all else, for it determines the course of your life [Proverbs 4:23]. Simple carnal thoughts and deeds might seem trivial to us but we should remember how it ended for Ananias and Sapphira, Judas Iscariot, King Saul, Hophni and Phineas and a host of other Biblical characters. By Jesus' death, we are redeemed and made righteous before God. Therefore, we but aspire to be Christ-like in all our daily endeavors.

The Shoes of Peace is the Believer's tranquility, the law of love your neighbour as thyself. A soldier wears a shoe to enable him walk in every terrain. On stony ground, coarse soil, mud, spiny surface, a soldier needs a solid footing, and this is why the commandment of love supersedes every other commandment. We must remember that it is by grace that we are saved, we can sidestep satan's tricks and devices if we remember what God did for us in John 3:16. We must not just exercise the gospel of peace, we must also spread it alike.

The Shield of Faith, this protects us from the unseen attacks. A soldier uses his shield to fend off flying arrows and slinging spears aimed at them. Sometimes the devil sends in our way doubts and fears to scare us and to shake our trust in God. Making us distrust in our God is one of the Devil's greatest tricks, remember the fall of man in the Garden of Eden and the temptation of Christ? The Devil makes us distrust in the Lord when He does not act immediately but as Christians, we must believe that our Father is reliable and trustworthy just like a soldier trusts in his shield to protect him from arrows that flies. So we must have faith in our God.

The Helmet of Salvation shows which party we belong to. Soldiers from different nations have distinguishing helmets to signify their allegiance or posse they belong to. If you do not have salvation through Christ, you cannot be identified with God's kingdom. Having salvation helps you enjoy the fullness of God. [2 Corinthians 10:5]. Secondly, the helmet protects the head, the Helmet of Salvations assures our protection and safety in Christ Jesus at all times.

Every weapon in the Amour of God are defensive, the Sword of the Spirit however is an offensive weapon which we can use as believers to combat the works and ploys of the devil. The Sword of the Spirit is the word of God; the Bible because the word of God is alive, active and sharp, even more than a double-edge sword. When Jesus was tempted by the devil, he rebuked the devil with the sword of the spirit.

Lastly, we are to empower ourselves in prayers, in all forms - supplications, intercession, thanksgiving, forgiveness etc. Soldiers are expected to keep the line of communication open with their Captain or Commander. God is our Commander; He has orders for us which He has carefully laid out in His word. We must keep talking to God through prayers.

Prayer Point:

- Heavenly Father, give me the understanding of what is true and right in everything I do.
- Furnish me with the fullness of your power and give me the grace to be a true soldier and stand at my post.

Chapter Seventeen

WAITING ON GOD

Rejoice with them that do rejoice, and weep with them that weep

Romans 12:12

Today, when we pray and do not receive and answers from God, we dissipate in our trust in God. Waiting patiently is an uncommon virtue in the body of Christ today. Do you remember how Job lost all but didn't waver his trust in God? How about Hannah, Abraham, etc.? Waiting on God is an ancient quality of the patriarchs and matriarchs of old. All these great characters in the Bible didn't lose their faith in God in their darkest times and even when it seemed pointless and hopeless.

We must know our God is a God of timing, punctuality and perfection, He does everything for a reason. God commanded us in Habakkuk 2:3 that "the vision is for an appointed time… though it lingers, wait for it, since it will surely come and not delay." Exodus 14:14 says "The Lord will fight for you; you only need to be still." Why trouble yourself when you have a faithful Father? Our concept of time is not the same with

God. However, He will never respond lately to your prayers. We must learn to conform ourselves with God's time rather than our own timing.

How do we wait on God? We can wait on God by being courageous, rejoicing in the hope that our Father in heaven is doing everything for our good even if we don't know His plans. We should wait believing and stay consistent in prayer. A persevering prayer moves the hands of God and compels Him to respond to us in this gracious nature.

We can wait on the Lord by studying His word and putting our hope in it. Remember the word of God is law and life. Many times, God is pruning out the enemies in our lives while we wait on Him, we might not know this but the God of the supernatural is in constant works in our lives so waiting on God requires a desirable amount of patience. While the children of Israel turned away from God in the wilderness, God was giving revelation to Moses on the mountain; maybe God is equipping your helper while you wait on him. Our God is a faithful God and He will not leave you forever in need of what is necessary to help you grow.

Prayer Points

- Holy Father, give me the strength to wait for your appointed time, I believe your appointed time is the best, give me the perseverance to await your response.

God be my salvation in times of distress, do not let me fail in my righteousness, let me walk and not be weary, let me run and not be tired.

Lord Jesus, help my unbelief and make me ever strong in your will.

Chapter Eighteen

EXPERIENCE THE POWER OF GOD

Psalm 147: 4-5

Jeremiah 10: 12-13

This is a very wonderful moment in our prayer journey and we are very glad that the mercies of the Lord has brought us this far. This is the time to experience the fullness of God and the demonstration of His greatness in our lives.

However, before we talk about experiencing the power of God, let us first acknowledge the power of God. How powerful do you think the Almighty is? If we have not experienced the power of God in our lives, let us look at how vast the universe, if we can't comprehend the vastness of the universe; the celestials, solar system let us look at the wonders within the earth, the creation of man, firmaments, nature and the likes. God has put wonders and perfection before our very eyes. He has designed an intricate system of interdependent bodies in one place - the universe. The creation of life is the greatest of all the signs of God's power.

The power of our God is simply unlimited. In fact, salvation, forgiveness, restoration, healing, love, grace, mercy, etc. that we enjoy are part of the display of the powers of God. Today, you are saying farewell to the confusions and troubles in your life. God has given you victory and from this day you are walking in the reality of this. Amen.

Prayer Points

- Dear Lord, I am grateful for the honor to be called your child and I thank You for the victory you have given me today.
- I pray that your power becomes evident more and more in my life and my testimony of Your grace endures forever in me in Jesus name.
- God, I commit myself to your plans, use me to do mighty works for the world to see your glory and power.
- From this day and for the rest of my life, make me walk in the reality of Your will. Amen.

CONCLUSION

PRAY WITHOUT CEASING!